Replacing Budgets With Palm Trees

Casey Ommen

ISBN-13:
978-1981490745

ISBN-10:
1981490744

2

3

Table of Contents

Flipping Your Way to Wealth

History Never Repeats Itself, Man Does

Mindset, Knowledge, Action

Intro

Budgets suck.

They are complicated and easily set us up for failure. There's the saying, <u>"We should only focus on the things we can control in life."</u>

When it comes to our expenses, we can't control the majority of them. Housing, insurance, and transportation are only a few of the basic necessities of modern life.

Add to that our food and household products, and nearly 80% of our expenses are locked in. This leaves us with the remaining 20% that we can actually try and control. Why do we spend so much of our time stressing over what we can squeeze out of these leftovers?

The concept of a budget sounds great but sticking to it is nearly impossible. Most of us are very familiar with the curve balls life loves to throw, many of them turn out to be large unexpected expenses: Broken appliances, car repairs, medical emergencies, vet bills, kids activities, weekend travels... The list is endless.

These are the cancers of all budgets. Unless you have a magic crystal ball, it is impossible to foresee these expenses every single month.

When these unexpected expenses hit us, and ruin our hard-thought-out budget, we get the urge to wish we could say: *"Screw the budget!"*

That is why I can't wait to introduce you to what we at KISSFinancials.com (Keep It Simple Stupid Financials) <u>created a tool that not only will replace your budget, but allow you to fully Organize, Automate, and Control your finances.</u>

See, if you truly want to be financially independent, you must have a working system in place that does <u>more than just calculate your expenses</u>. Soon you will see for yourself just how we were able to replace the ancient old budget once and for all.

The shaded cone below represents the percentage of information we tend to remember after a two-week period of time.

Cone of Learning

After 2 weeks we tend to remember		Nature of Involvement
90% of what we say and do	**Doing the Real Thing**	**Active**
	Simulating the Real Experience	
	Doing a Dramatic Presentation	
70% of what we say	**Giving a Talk**	
	Participating in a Discussion	
50% of what we hear and see	**Seeing it Done on Location**	**Passive**
	Watching a Demonstration	
	Looking at an Exhibit Watching a Demonstration	
	Watching a Movie	
30% of what we see	**Looking at Pictures**	
20% of what we hear	**Hearing Words**	
10% of what we read	**Reading**	

(Source: Cone of Learning adapted from Edgar Dale, 1969)

The diagram shows the five forms of action we take and how they determine the amount of information we will remember. These actions are: <u>reading, hearing, seeing, saying (speaking), and doing</u>.

It's unfortunate but it teaches us that we remember only _10% of what we read_. Now slow down this doesn't mean stop reading, with your help we can achieve the full 90%, let me explain.

To start I have placed many "golden nuggets" (= key principles and methods) throughout this book in various forms. In order for you to remember and apply them, make sure that you highlight, screenshot, and store those nuggets when you come across them.

As you move up the pyramid, you will see that we remember only _20% of what we hear_. Our busy lives reduce our quiet time drastically giving us little time to truly sit down and read. A free audible version will be available online soon. This way you can listen to the book when you go for a walk or are driving to work.

The _Cone of Learning_ says that we remember 30% of what we see. This is because our brain processes visuals easier and, in turn, our memory benefits more from pictures than from words.

Our daily content overload on social media and the internet is immense. No wonder our eyes tend to glaze over words and focus instead only on the visuals. That is why I have laid out as many drawings for you as possible.

At *50%* in the pyramid, you will see that a combination of *both hearing and seeing* leads to greater learning results. Words and pictures alone can provide only so much value. If you want to understand something fully, some form of live or recorded demonstration is required.

The *Cone of Learning* pyramid is broken up into two parts: passive and active. Once you finished reading this book (passively), it is up to you to take action and achieve the full 90% potential.
For it is these actions that will allow you to take control of your finances.

A story is often rich in metaphors that teach us lessons about life. A good story can help us understand ourselves and the world around us on a deeper level. Once we connect emotionally with such a story the lessons become easier to apply to our own life.

To illustrate the lessons I hope you will gain from this book, let me share with you a short story from the bestseller *"The Alchemist"*.

"You must always know what it is that you want," the old king had said. The boy knew and was now working toward it...

He was proud of himself. He had learned some important things, like how to deal in crystal, and about the language without words… and about omens. One afternoon he had seen a man at the top of the hill, complaining that it was impossible to find a decent place to get something to drink after such a climb. The boy, accustomed to recognizing omens, spoke to the merchant.

"Let's sell tea to the people who climb the hill."

"Lots of places sell tea around here," the merchant said.

"But we could sell tea in crystal glasses. The people will enjoy the tea and want to buy the glasses. I have been told that <u>beauty is the great seducer of men</u>."

The merchant didn't respond, but that afternoon, after saying his prayers and closing the shop, he invited the boy to sit with him and share his hookah, that strange pipe used by the Arabs.

"What is it you're looking for?" asked the old merchant.

"I've already told you. I need to buy my sheep back, so I have to earn the money to do so."

The merchant put some new coals in the hookah and inhaled deeply.

"*I' ve had this shop for thirty years. I know good crystal from bad, and everything else there is to know about the crystal. I know its dimensions and how it behaves. If we serve tea in crystal, the shop is going to expand. And then I' ll have to change my way of life.* "

"*Well, isn' t that good?*"

"*I' m already used to the way things are. Before you came, I was thinking about how much time I had wasted in the same place, while my friends had moved on, and either went bankrupt or did better than they had before. It made me very depressed. Now, I can see that it hasn' t been too bad. The shop is exactly the size I always wanted it to be. I don' t want to change anything because I don' t know how to deal with change. I' m used to the way I am.* "

14

The boy didn't know what to say. The old man continued, "You have been a real blessing to me. Today, I understand something I didn't see before: every blessing ignored becomes a curse. I don't want anything else in life. But you are forcing me to look at wealth and at horizons I have never known. Now that I have seen them, and now that I see how immense my possibilities are, I am going to feel worse than I did before you arrived. Because I know the things I should be able to accomplish, and I don't want to do so…"

They went on smoking the pipe for a while as the sun began to set. They were conversing in Arabic, and the boy was proud of himself for being able to do so. There had been a time when he thought that his sheep could teach him everything he needed to know about the world. But they could never have taught him Arabic.

There are probably other things in the world that the sheep can't teach me, thought the boy as he regarded the old merchant. All they ever do, really, is look for food and water. And maybe it wasn't that they were teaching me, but that I was learning from them.

"Maktub," the merchant said, finally.

"What does that mean?"

"You would have to have been born an Arab to understand," he answered. "But in your language, it would be something like "It is written." And, as he smothered the coals in the hookah, he told the boy that he could begin to sell tea in the crystal glasses. Sometimes, there's just no way to hold back the river…

Before long, the news spread, and a great many people began to climb the hill to see the shop that was doing something new in a trade that was so old. Other shops were opened that served tea in crystal, but they weren't at the top of a hill, and they had little business. Eventually, the merchant had to hire two more employees. He began to import enormous quantities of tea along with his crystal, and his shop was sought out by men and women with a thirst for things new.

(Coelho, Paulo. *The Alchemist*, 2014, pp. 58-62)

This book will help you crystallize your financial goals and ambitions in life. It will explain why neither wandering aimlessly nor standing still will bring you closer to changing your financial situation.

In order to act purposefully, you will learn the principles and tools that are fundamental to realizing your financial goals. The following pages show you the path to a new definition of wealth.

If you seek the clarity and tools to regain control over your finances, change is imperative. Be prepared to leave your idea of "budgeting" behind, for it is ancient in its approach and limited in its value.

You Are

Your Only Limit

Letting Go

Debt isn't something anyone should take lightly because it doesn't magically sort itself out. It takes time and persistence to kick old habits out the window, and replace them with a mindset geared towards financial independence.

<u>In fact, your mindset may very well be the most important because it's what we choose to store in our mind that holds us back – or liberates us</u>.

A hunter tries to catch a monkey that is stealing food from his town. Even after endless chasing of the monkey, the hunter still has no luck because the monkey is quite clever: It runs fast, climbs, and jumps from tree to tree. The hunter begins to feel it is impossible for him to capture the animal.

Just as the hunter is about to give up, a wise old man from town walks up to him. The old man advises him to get a rope, a coconut, and some sugar and peanuts. Following the old man's instructions, the hunter cuts a portion off the top of the coconut, leaving a small hole in the center just big enough to fit a monkey's hand. He then places sugar-coated peanuts inside the hole and ties the coconut to a tree with the rope.

At the end of the day, the hunter goes home to get some rest. When the hunter wakes up the next morning, he goes to check on his coconut.

Just as the old wise man predicted, the monkey is there, running around the tree in a circle with its hand stuck inside the coconut!

The monkey had stuck its hand in the coconut to get the sugary peanuts and now holds on to them with his fist. The problem is that its fist is bigger than the hole in the coconut. If only the monkey were willing to let go of the sweet peanuts and open its hand, he would be able to run free.

The moral of the story: The hunter, who had been sleeping the whole night, was not the one who caught the monkey. <u>The monkey imprisoned itself because it was unwilling to let go.</u>

If you are stuck financially, stop making the same financial mistakes over and over again. Learn to let go of old habits.

"You don't have to cling to a mistake just because you spent a lot of time making it."

Negativity paralyzes us from moving forward in life. If you want to improve your financial situation, learn to take responsibility for past decisions and the consequences that resulted from those decisions. Acknowledge that neither the economy, nor the government, nor your boss is to blame.

As difficult as it is to face our own shortcomings, accepting responsibility will liberate you in two ways: <u>One, you'll start taking charge of your life which is empowering in itself. And two, now that you understand your past, are able to take the right steps in sorting out your current and future financial situation</u>.

"All of you were given two great gifts: your mind and your time. It is up to you to do what you please with both. With each dollar bill that enters your hand, you and only you have the power to determine your destiny. Spend it foolishly, you choose to be poor. Spending it on liabilities, you join the middle class. Invest it in your mind and learn how to acquire assets and you will be choosing wealth as your goal and your future. The choice is yours and only yours. Every day with every dollar, you decide to be rich, poor or middle class."

- Kiyosaki, Robert T. *Rich Dad, Poor Dad*, 2004, p. 179.

Materialistic Change

Many of us see materialistic change as *the* answer to happiness. To some degree, that is understandable because buying a new item delights us and we are joyous in that moment. We truly believe that the new kitchen table or new toolbox was the last missing piece in our happiness puzzle. Fast forward three weeks later, however, we feel just as restless and the kitchen table no longer excites us.

Unfortunately, the American dream is moving further away from what it used to represent and instead is becoming more and more materialistic. <u>We have taken our desire for "stuff" to a point at which we fill our garages with unnecessary gadgets until we find ourselves running out of space.</u>

Instead of raising the level of our emotional and spiritual well-being, we tend to dig ourselves deeper into debt because we buy more physical "stuff". So why is it that we struggle to understand that long-term happiness doesn't come with the products we buy?

To understand how big of a problem our accumulating things have become, look at the below statistics about the clutter in our lives:

1. There are 300,000 items in the average American home. (**LA Times**)

2. The average size of the American home has nearly tripled over the past 50 years. (**NPR**)

3. 25% of people with two-car garages don't have room to park cars inside their garage, and 32% have room for only one vehicle. (**U.S. Department of Energy**)

4. The United States has more than 50,000 storage facilities – that is five times the number of Starbucks stores! Currently, there are 7.3 square feet of self-storage space available for every man, woman, and child in the nation. Thus, it is physically possible for all Americans to stand under the total canopy of self-storage roofing – at the same time. (**SSA**)

5. 3.1% of the world's children live in America but they own 40% of the toys consumed globally. (**UCLA**)

6. British research found that the average 10-year-old owns 238 toys but plays with just 12 of them every day. (**The Telegraph**)

7. Americans spend more on shoes, jewelry, and watches ($100 billion) than on higher education. (**Psychology Today**)

8. The average American throws away 65 pounds of clothing per year. (**Huffington Post**)

9. Women spend more than eight years of their lives shopping. (**The Daily Mail**)

10. Over the course of our lifetime, we will spend a total of 3,680 hours (153 days) searching for misplaced items. That adds up to nine lost items every day or 198,743 in a lifetime. Phones, keys, sunglasses, and paperwork are at the top the list. (**The Daily Mail**)

(Source: Beker, Joshua. "21 Surprising Statistics That Reveal How Much Stuff We Actually Own." *Becoming Minimalist*, 25 Aug. 2017)

"You can be rich by having more than you need, or by needing less than you have." Jim Mott.

This mindset shift is tricky because every day, we are bombarded with ads telling us how a certain product will make us happier, cooler, or more socially acceptable. Whether it's the shiny new car on a billboard or the latest gadget online – every ad aims at our impulse to buy, to consume us until we breathe our last breath.

But the positive effects of materialist change are almost always temporary. The thrill that comes with each of our purchases inevitably wears off.

That is why we are running in circles. We buy more stuff to try and fill this insatiable urge inside of us and completely miss the point. It is not material possessions that we crave but the connection with other people, a sense of belonging and purpose. Those are the driving forces behind our purchases.

Break free from impulsive shopping sprees to "treat yourself" or else the things that you own will end up owning you. When you understand that the satisfaction you get from such purchases is a short-lived illusion of happiness, then you are on your way to financial freedom.

It is important to understand that happiness in life doesn't automatically increase with more money, and certainly not with more material possessions.

"Money often makes obvious our tragic human flaws. Money often puts a spotlight on what we do not know. That is why, all too often, a person who comes into a sudden windfall of cash – let's say an inheritance, a pay raise or lottery winnings – soon returns to the same financial mess, if not worse than the mess they were in before they received the money. Money only accentuates the cash-flow pattern running in your head." - Kiyosaki, Robert T. Rich Dad, Poor Dad, 2004, pp. 59.

The Beatles wisely sang that money can't buy us love. As much as some women go crazy over a new Chanel bag, it cannot (and should not) serve as a token of love.

For women, looking past the empty promises of beautifying products is very hard. Clever ad campaigns single out women into thinking that when they continuously splurge on beautifying products, they too can become truly beautiful. <u>Here today, gone tomorrow, all on a whim of an industry.</u>

No wonder we keep buying more stuff. Not because we need it, but because we long for a deeper form of change, a change from within. The kind of change that is permanent.

See, the world never truly changes; it is your mindset that creates and shapes the change you see and experience. Internal change is what will make the biggest impact on your life, and a different mindset will not only shape your life but can also line your pockets.

<u>Self-awareness is *the* most important ingredient for change from within.</u> Once you understand which forces (internal and external) drive your purchase decisions, you will see your financial struggles in a new light. You are now one crucial step closer to fixing them.

<u>You are your cause, and your solution – you are the one who has to change.</u>

"So much of what makes us wealthy is free. Remember what Sir John Templeton told us: the secret to wealth is gratitude. It's not just what we achieve or accomplish. It's what we appreciate. It's not just the adventure of the cruise. It's what we take the time to enjoy. You can find an adventure and joy in those you love, in the dancing eyes of your children or the joyous faces of those you love. There are jackpots everywhere if you wake up to the beauty of your life today. So don't vow to someday get beyond scarcity; start beyond it realize how lucky you are and all the wealth you possess in love, joy opportunities, health, friends, and family. Don't get rich. Start rich."

– Robbins, Tony. Money: Master the Game, 2014, p. 347

Success Without Fulfilment

"Success without fulfillment is the ultimate failure."
- Tony Robbins

The stories of overnight success will always be the carrot on the end of the stick. They will never replace the sense of fulfillment we have when we work towards things that really matter to us. Whether you start a business, get rich, or eliminate your debt: If the results of your hard work hasn't fulfilled you, you have failed.

The journey to success – however you define it for your own life – is a long one. At times, it may be rocky and seem endless. So, it is important that you spend your time and efforts wisely and on tasks that bring you closer to what fulfills you.

<u>It's figuring out what brings joy and happiness into your own life and the lives of others, and acting accordingly.</u> Focus on figuring out what your vision for your life is, your purpose, your *why*, and then turn it into reality.

Choosing a career that supports our long-term goals is crucial but most of us realize only later in life that we are indeed on the wrong corporate ladder or hustling in an industry not in line with our values and beliefs.

We stay put in our jobs or industries because we believe that it is too late to start over. Or worse because our manager promises us a raise, a promotion or even a share of the company if we work hard for another five to ten years.

ONe day If you woRK HaRd foR Me I will HaNd this Business oveR To you

The issue with <u>getting caught in the promises that are "sold" to us is that they are beyond our control.</u> Managers can't even guarantee job stability for their own positions, let alone yours, and yet we postpone the job search till "later".

We think we can always change jobs or move to another city *later*, and that dream of a happy future keeps us grinding every day. If only we understood that it is our desire for *security* that really pins us down! <u>We believe that if we stay where we are, our income is safe, our job is safe, our lifestyle is safe...</u>

But your lifestyle isn't "safe" because the job that generates your income supporting your lifestyle is beyond your control. If you get sacked tomorrow, your world will most likely come crashing down on you. This is why it is important that you complete this book and take action. For these simplistic techniques will assist you on how to finally be in control of your financial situation and ultimately your life.

$75,000

I have started this reading with the notion that true happiness doesn't come from money, but from the people and moments that have personal value and deeper meaning. This is not to say that money isn't important. To a degree, it is indeed connected to our happiness.

A study conducted by Princeton University's Woodrow Wilson School several years ago came to an obvious conclusion: people need money to be happy. But the underlining question is exactly how much?

<u>The magic number of money-based happiness is $75,000.</u> That's good news for those of us who aren't insanely rich because with a steady job in a prospering economy, this is an achievable amount.

It's enough money to take care of our most basic needs and still have money left for the things we enjoy. To be able to pay for our doctor's appointments, eat better quality food, travel on holidays. Being able to financially get ourselves to the point where we don't have to worry about making ends meet every month.

With anything more than $75,000, our level of money-based happiness begins to plateau. The study suggests that there are two different kinds of happiness. The first kind is happiness on a day-to-day basis, influenced by mood changes, temporary stress levels, and feelings.

Emotional changes are based on events which happen to everyone, regardless of their wealth. So, making more than $75,000 a year will have no impact on this type of happiness because you still have to deal with bad weather, a sad story, or a stressful day at work.

The second type, long-term happiness, relates to the overall level of satisfaction with your life. This type directly depends on your life, on where you live, what you do, and how you see your situation. Unlike the first type, long-term happiness does depend on money beyond that $75,000 threshold. The more money you make, the more you are likely to feel that your life is exactly how you want it to be.

$75,000 a year provides stability and keeps you above the level of scarcity. It makes you comfortable and satisfied but you won't be immune to life's everyday challenges.

Obviously, money matters. It influences how you see your life and it can even help you achieve fulfillment. Although my primary mission is to enable you to get out of debt, I also aim to help you achieve this $75,000 income mark.

Once you replace your budget with your own *Wealthy Palm Tree* as outlined shortly in the next section, you will realize how little time it takes to follow this method. This will inevitably allow you to focus more effort on increasing your income; which is another thing a budget does a great job blinding us from.

Minding

Your Own

Business

Running Your Warehouse

The common notion these days is that we can quit the rat race only if we start our own business or invent a product and star on *Shark Tank*. With all the "entrepreneurial busy-ness" in our society, we completely fail to realize that we already own our own business: our personal life.

This is by far the most important business we will ever run. <u>If you want to create wealth in your life, you must begin by "Minding Your Own Business",</u> a term used by Robert Kiyosaki in *Rich Dad, Poor Dad*. Many of the investing principles that are required in running a successful business are similar to running a successful personal life.

<u>To a large degree, running our personal life can be compared to running a warehouse.</u> For you to succeed, you need to put on your "warehouse manager hat" each time you make a financial decision in your life, big or small.

Let's dive into what running a successful warehouse/personal life looks like. The *basic expenses* to run both your life and a warehouse are your mortgage/rent, your insurances (home, personal, and vehicle), and your utilities (internet, mobile phone, gas, electricity, water).

If you have a partner, your stakes in your warehouse will be shared 50/50. If you have kids, they are part of the deal as well (consider them your "interns") and add them to the expenses.

To keep our life operational, we have to buy inventory and supplies regularly. Depending on our routine, we might go to stores weekly or even daily. For it takes a lot of work to organize, clean and maintain our warehouse. To say the least it's a big job and never for one person alone, especially when you realize that you lack expertise in certain areas.

Marcus Lemonis, entrepreneur and investor, stars in the TV show "The Profit" on CNBC and partners up with small businesses to help them overcome their struggles. If you haven't watched his show, tune in! Lemonis breaks every company's business model up into three categories: <u>People, Product, and Process.</u>

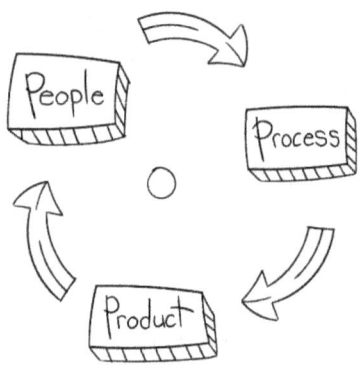

People - As you know, you need to have the right people working for you to be a successful long-term entrepreneur. Even more critical though, those people have to have the right roles in your warehouse. So, knowing your partner's and kids' strengths and weaknesses are key when you delegate tasks.

Product - Learn to buy your inventory and equipment from the right suppliers. This is important because knowing *what to buy from whom* will save you a lot of money. Also, knowing how to find customers to (re)sell your unused or stranded inventory to maximize profits.

Process - The efficiency of your warehouse/life is fundamental to getting things done. From experience, this is the area people need the most help. That is why the majority of this book focuses on helping you create a process that will *keep* your finances *organized, automated and under control.*

Statistics show that 8 out of 10 businesses fail within the first 18 months of existence. I believe the number is so high because those 8 business owners potentially never cultivated the entrepreneurial mindset necessary to run their *private lives* successfully first, let alone a separate business.

"If you are going to build the Empire State Building, the first thing you need to do is dig a deep hole and pour a strong foundation. If you are going to build a home in the suburbs, all you need to do is pour a 6-inch slab of concrete. Most people, in their drive to get rich, are trying to build an Empire State Building on a 6-inch slab."

- *Kiyosaki, Robert T. Rich Dad, Poor Dad, 2004, pp. 51.*

Replacing Budgets
with
Palm Trees

When it comes to getting your financial situation under control, the common notion is that you have to start with a budget. The good old Excel spreadsheet which breaks up your expenses into sections such as housing, transport, insurance, food, children, entertainment, loans, taxes, and personal care.

I agree that breaking up your expenses this way is a very logical thing to do. What about when it comes to the math part of a budget? Out of all the subjects in school, statistics show that math was probably one of your less successful subjects.

However, let's assume you correctly categorized and calculated your monthly expenses. Now, the second step of budgeting involves you "guessing" what next month's expenses will be. However, this involves not only more calculations but increases the possibility of errors.

Worse still, your frustration and stress levels increase proportionally to the time you spend hammering out the numbers. In the end, the budget-guessing-game leaves you with only halfway accurate figures upon which you base your spending for next month.

The chances are high that you end up tweaking your budget mid-month to account for all the unexpected expenses you could not anticipate (or simply forgot).

This is because life throws many financial curveballs our way, and usually at the worst times possible. In those moments, the temptation is high to revert back to old habits and stop caring about our finances. So, you quit.

Budgeting for a family is another story altogether. Your kids and spouse have to be on board for it to work. Who hasn't had one of those late-night discussions on how we spend our money, who earns more, who is entitled to spend a greater portion of the joint income.

It's unfortunate that finances are the leading cause of stress in a relationship. That is why a simplified, straight cut method is needed. So, then your family can tackle your financial situation without lumps in your throats.

In essence, traditional budgeting doesn't seem like the method of choice if you want to get a handle on your finances and value your relationships. The process of how to create and stick to a perfect budget is filled with too many gray areas.

We have finally reached the part of this book where I am going to reveal to you what we at KISSFinacials.com call the *Wealthy Palm Tree* method. It's *easy to understand and apply,* and fits in well with today's extremely visual, technologically advanced society.

My personal "Aha moment" came when I realized that <u>a budget only focuses on "how much" we are spending but not (more importantly) "how" we are spending our money.</u> Think about deodorant or shampoo, for example. We all have to buy it, and most of us keep paying premium prices at a retail store or worse Walgreens, when we should be buying larger quantities and receiving wholesale pricing.

Saving goes beyond the supermarket though. I'll say it now: <u>If you don't have an eBay account, you will keep throwing money out the window.</u> eBay came at a time when people were still skeptical of purchasing items with their credit cards online. It wasn't until Amazon when people began to be more comfortable with online purchases.

Each week I buy items on eBay and resell them on Amazon for a consistent profit. This is possible because there are still millions of consumers out there who don't know how to source products at the best price.

Let's get on with it, prepare to say "Bye" to that budget and Excel sheet once and for all.

The layout of the palm tree is based on a technique called mind mapping which has been around for centuries, known to have been invented by the famous Leonardo da Vinci.

Your *Wealthy Palm Tree* will consist of three sections: Income, Assets, and Expenses:

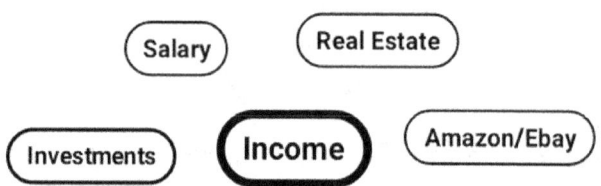

Income represents the *palm leaves*. Just like any tree, your *Wealthy Palm Tree* will start off with one or only very few leaves, providing you little shade. But, over time, your leaves will multiply and grow until one day they provide you with a wide shaded area under which you can retire.

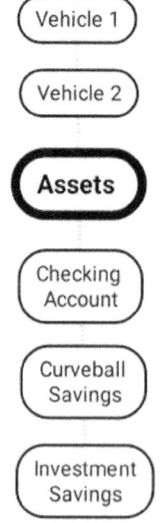

Assets represent *the trunk* which stabilizes the palm tree. Over time, as more water is absorbed into the trunk and more assets are purchased, your *Wealthy Palm Tree* will grow sturdier and taller.

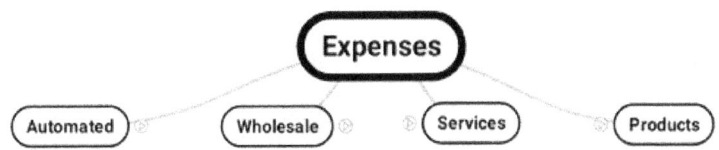

Expenses represent *the roots* of your tree. They absorb all the water and nutrients which help your tree not only survive but grow. Every expense falls into one of the four categories.

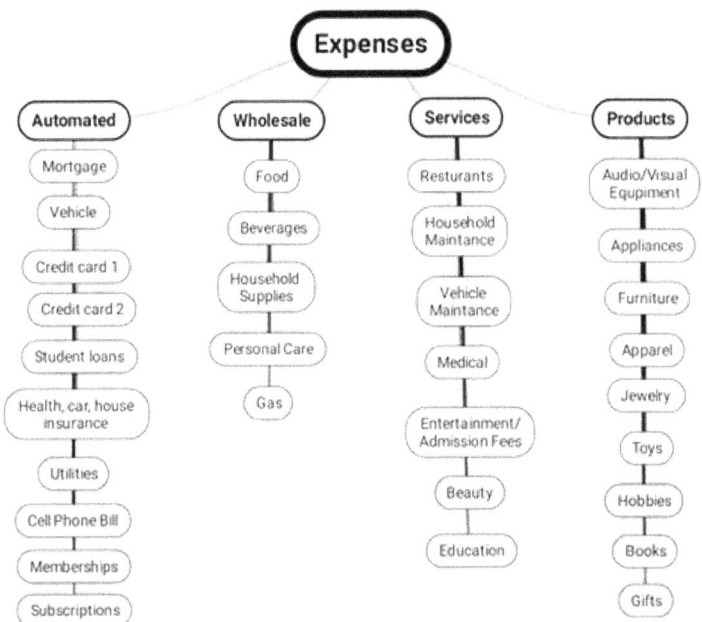

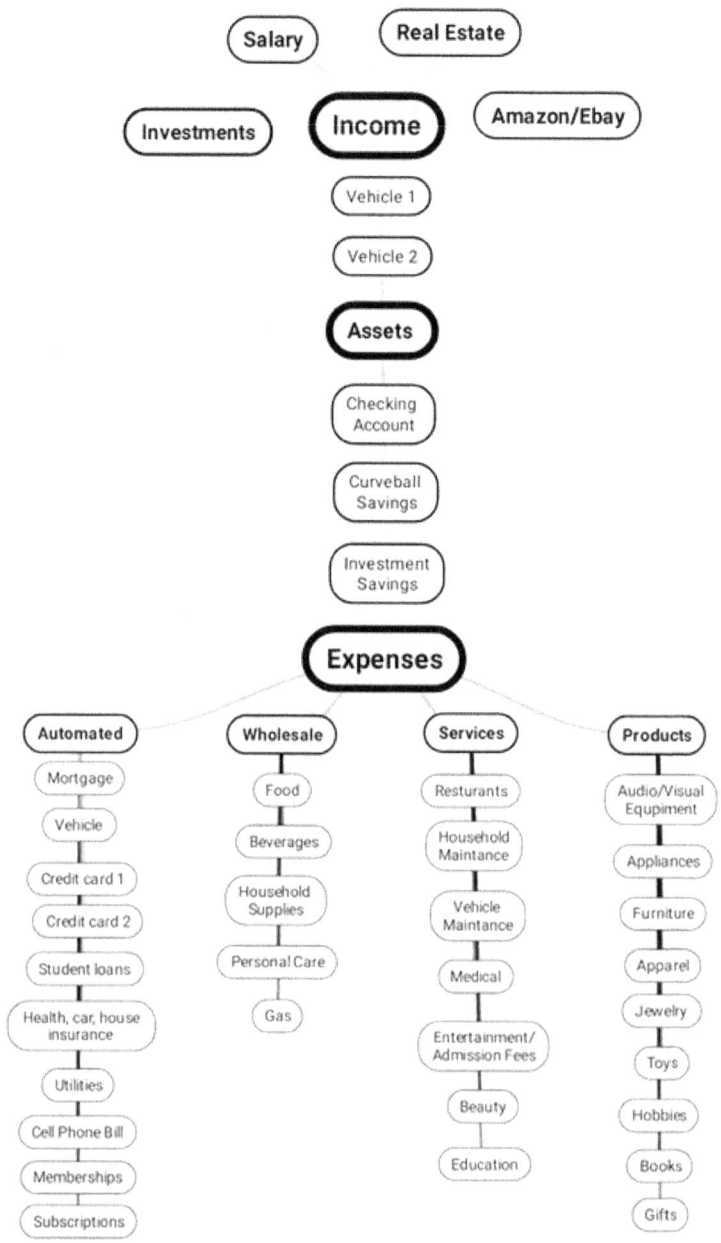

(Take a picture or screenshot of the Wealthy Palm Tree with your phone to refer back to)

You will notice that most of your reoccurring expenses, i.e. expenses for things you need to run your everyday life, make up the left two bubbles within automated and wholesale expenses.

Those colored in _blue_ represent your debt, or, as Dave Ramsey would say, your "snowballs". As you would imagine, palm trees and snow don't go well together. That is why we want to eliminate all the snowballs as we can from our expenses.

I assume that the debt you have taken on isn't "good" debt (debt which generates more income for you). Therefore, we won't go further into the difference of good debt and bad debt till further down the road.

A little easier and more interesting than staring at an Excel spreadsheet, I hope?

The most valuable part of this whole concept is that you can click on each _bubble_ and enter any text, URL links, and even pictures to store your individual information for that particular bubble.

Let's take your insurance expenses, for example. In the _Health, Vehicle, House Insurance_ bubbles, you will insert the web links to your insurance agents' sites, their contact information, and any notes regarding your insurance policies.

In the *Cell Phone Bill* bubble, you would note which plan you have and your login details for your online account. For the *Vehicle* bubbles, you will save a copy of the title information, your mechanic's contact details, and when the oil and filters were last replaced.

The method is the same for every other bubble of your *Wealthy Palm Tree* – you can select the most important pieces of information that you will need to remember so when something comes up at a later date, you don't waste hours searching for a paper you threw in a random drawer eight months ago.

<u>You see, when it comes to getting a handle on your finances, organizing all the "moving parts" (your contracts and information, for example) is half the battle.</u> This is why the *Wealthy Palm Tree* has provided so much value to individuals, because it becomes such a customizable organizational tool as well.

In the coming pages of the *Three Spending Commandments*, we will break down the *Expenses* section further into *Automated*, *Wholesale*, *Services*, and *Product Expenses*. These four sub-categories are important because, once fully outlined, based on your financial situation, you will see clearly where your hard-earned dollars go every month. But first we must focus on how we are going to automate our banking.

Automating Your Banking

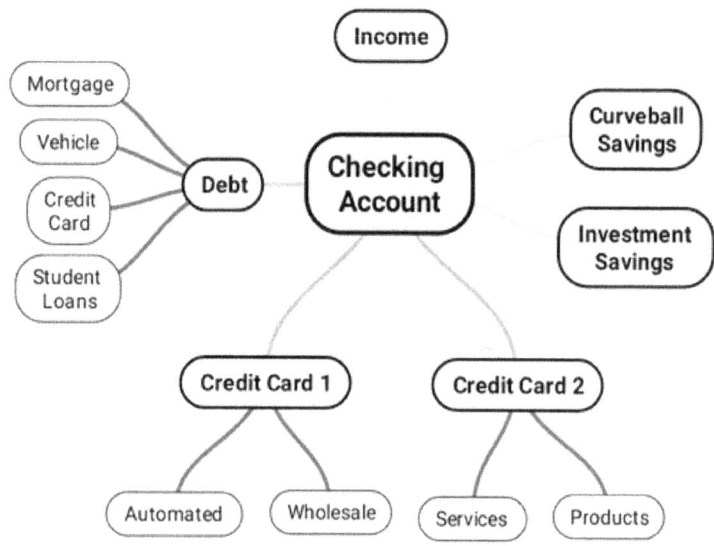

Here is where people begin to complicate things. In the interest of keeping things as simple as possible, the above chart is color-coded to match your *Wealthy Palm Tree*. <u>Green is for your *Income*, orange for your *Assets*, red for your *Expenses*, and blue for your snowballs of debt.</u>

The idea of this chart is that all your money will flow around clockwise. Let's start with *Income*. For many of us, our salary is the only source of income that will be deposited into our checking account. (Hopefully, very soon you will be getting a little Amazon and/or eBay check that will flow into this as well.)

There should be two *savings* attached to your checking account, to begin with. The first one will be your *Curveball Savings*, aka your emergency fund, and second, your *Investing Savings*.

We will start by cushioning your *Curveball Savings* account with $1,000. Once you have paid off all your debt, you will want to cushion this account further with up to 6 months' worth of expenses at the least.

For your *Investing Savings* account, we will automatically drip 10% of your income into this account. This money should be understood as capital, aka cash on hand, and should be used for investment opportunities you may want to act on quickly. If you don't have cash on hand, this is impossible, so building up an investment savings account is important. It also teaches you the value of paying yourself first.

The next section of the flow chart is your *Credit Cards*. You will have no more than two credit cards. *Credit Card One* is for all your *Automated* expenses and *Wholesale* purchases. Because the *Automated* expenses get taken out without your intervention, you will only physically use this on the large *Wholesale* purchases when you buy in bulk. This will be the card with the most dollars spent.

Credit Card Two is to be used for all other daily *Services* and *Products* you purchase, i.e. the smaller items. This card should be your main area of focus because the majority of the purchases you buy with this card are oftentimes not necessary (aka impulse purchases). Be creative and cut the costs before you make any purchases with this card.

When it comes to your *Debit Card*, only use it for cash purchases. Don't link this card to your other purchases because you don't want to worry about potential overdraft charges or constantly check how much you have in your checking account. Using two credit cards allows you to streamline your banking and gain a better overview of your expenses.

In addition to your *Wealthy Palm Tree*, the *Automated Banking Chart* gives you an easy overview of how much you spend per category (Credit Card One and Credit Card Two). All you have to do is keep an eye on the total amounts of the credit cards at the end of each month striving to lower your expenses every month.

So, at the end of each month all you will have to do is, log into your mobile banking account, look at the amount you were able to save in your checking account, and decide how much of your smallest debt snowball you are able to pay off.

Yes, we are going to use the snowball technique to pay off your debt. In the grand scheme of things, this strategy is the most simplified way of paying off your debt. You eliminate as many moving parts as you can.

When it comes to student loans, I would agree with the traditional view that you should always pay off your credit cards first. The difference in interest rates is just too high (student loan at 6% vs. a maxed-out credit card at 16%).

This section will be much easier to grasp and complete once you follow the online videos at KISSFinancials.com. Just remember the key principle of running a successful warehouse/life is eliminating as many moving variables as you can.

Fully automating your banking along with having your finances organized will put you a head of 90% of individuals today.

"Do today what others won't, so you can live tomorrow like others can't."

Three

Spending

Commandments

1st Commandment — LIMIT ALL SERVICES

2ND Commandment — Purchase Wholesale

3RD Commandment — Source Below Market Value

Products vs. Services

We spend money on one of two things, a *product or a service.* Being able to distinguish between these two kinds of expenses determines your long-term financial success (i.e. building wealth).

A *product expense* is any purchase where you receive a physical item in return for your money; it is something you take home. In some cases, you can resell this product at a later date if you want to (e.g. headphones, a TV, or your car).

A *service expense,* on the other hand, is an intangible experience you receive in exchange for your money; you cannot resell this at a later point to recoup your money. The majority of your purchases are most likely service-related (e.g. your cell phone contract, gym membership, or health insurance).

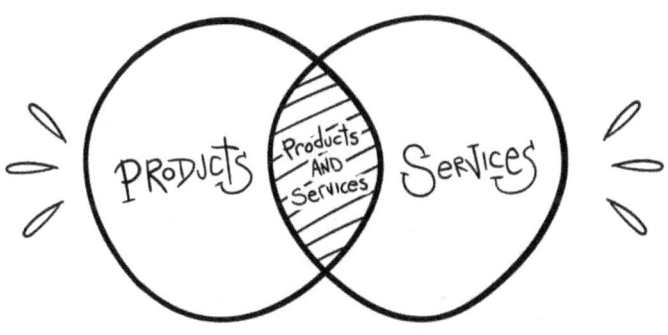

Now if we make a Venn Diagram of products and services, you would notice an overlap, as there is a large number of product/service businesses out there.

Examples range from restaurants to car repair shops and plumbing companies which all provide a service and a product of some sort at the same time (food, spare parts, a new pipe). However, almost all of these will fall under the service category because you cannot resell your leftovers from the restaurant or the oil you just had put in your car.

There are two quotes we will focus on in the upcoming sections:

Quote One:

"Most people spend and make themselves poor. If you are going to be rich, you need to know how to spend to make yourself rich."
- Trump, Donald, and Robert T Kiyosaki.
Why We Want You To Be Rich, 2006, p. 238

That is what makes this quote so interesting. It doesn't say: "Know how to *invest* to make yourself rich." It says, "Know how to *spend* to make yourself rich." The reason is, because as much as 80% of our expenses fall into the *spending* category. With a percentage this high, you need to make sure you aren't consistently leaving any money on the table.

Quote Two:

"You have to make the shift from being a consumer in the economy to becoming an owner – and you do it by becoming an investor."
– Robbins, Tony. Money:
Master the Game, 2014, p. 6

When we spend 80% of our money on expenses, we fall into the consumer category. But what about the remaining 20%? See, <u>a consumer only spends his money, with no intention of ever selling the items he buys.</u>

<u>An investor, however, spends his money with the mindset that, come the day when he doesn't need that item anymore, he can sell it for equal or greater value.</u>

With this knowledge in mind, let's proceed to the "*Three Spending Commandments*" which are designed to help you make smarter buying decisions to optimize any savings. Ultimately allowing you to take control of your spending.

First Commandment:
Limit All Services

Limit as many service expenses as you possibly can! Why? You can't resell your services to get back a portion of the money you spent on them.

<u>Every time you spend $1 of your hard-earned money, you will receive $0 of it back.</u> Examples of services are: all kinds of insurances, utilities, memberships, hotel rooms, etc.

Look at your *Wealthy Palm Tree* and find the two *Service* expense bubbles. The first category contains *Automated* expenses, this step is very simple.

The objective is to identify all your automated expenses that are being taken out of, or can be taken out of, your credit card or checking account automatically – your hands-off expenses.

Go to your bank account and identify those "lingering" monthly charges for subscriptions you signed up for ages ago and completely forgot about. <u>These are the culprits you are after. Once you have identified them, cancel all those services that you don't use or can easily live without.</u>

For the services/subscriptions that you want to keep, compare competitors and switch providers or negotiate with your current service providers to bring the costs down. That goes especially for insurances, phone and internet plans as these are reoccurring monthly expenses you can easily reduce. Saving just $100 a month by simply comparing providers adds up to $1,200 a year.

Now let's address the elephant in the room: the *debt snowballs*. This is why your bad debt is in the automated/service expense category:

Even though your house and car are physical *products*, you are still paying the bank or dealership a percentage for their service of lending you money to live in your house and drive your car. Therefore, until both car and house are paid off, you are not the sole owner of either of them.

When you make the last payment on your car loan, this *blue expense* will turn into an *orange asset*. When you pay off your credit card debt, this *blue expense* will drop off your *Wealthy Palm Tree* forever. These are the goals we strive for to achieve financial freedom.

When items change their position don't forget to keep track of the progress and add any notes/documents you might need to refer back to later.

The neat thing about when you have completed the *Automated* expense bubble, you don't have to touch it for the next six to twelve months. It's like going to the dentist: You get your teeth cleaned twice a year, that's it.

When you add up your mortgage, car and credit card debts, the *Automated* expense bubble can make up nearly half your expenses. So, it is important that you know what you are paying for and find ways to eliminate as many of these expenses as you can.

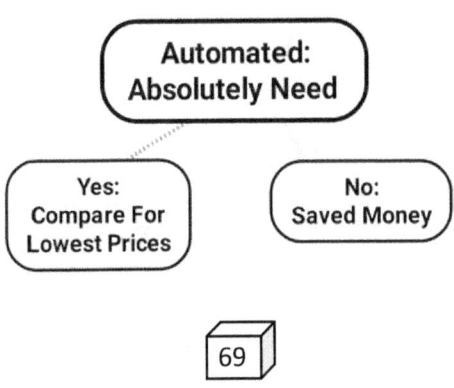

The other bubble in your *Wealthy Palm Tree* that falls under the first spending commandment is *Services (restaurants, entertainment, travel, maintenance)*.

The more creative you get, the more you will be able to save on these service bubbles. If you don't think of yourself as the creative type of person, especially when it comes to saving, then surf the web for creative ideas that are already out there.

YouTube videos, Pinterest, and blogs on life hacks are great sources. We will break down more in-depth ways to save on each of these bubbles individually online. (KISSFinacials.com)

You will be surprised how many things you can do yourself instead of paying professionals for their services. Watch a tutorial on a barista course and treat yourself to great café-style coffee at home.

When the mechanic says the filter of your car needs to be replaced, take a picture of that filter and buy a new one on eBay at a fraction of the cost he would charge.

Another such category is *travel*. Think of costs for hotels, gas, and eating out. This can get expensive, especially when you have kids and you take them to sporting events every weekend.

Unless you have a good strategy, you'll have a huge expense on your hands. Instead of booking the usual hotel room, register with Airbnb at a fraction of the price without losing out on any convenience or comfort.

Another advantage of Airbnb over hotels is you get to stock up your host's refrigerator to cook your own meals instead of feeling like you have to go out to eat every meal.

You can even double dip and use Airbnb to rent out your own home for the period you are away.

"By failing to prepare, you are preparing to fail."
- Benjamin Franklin

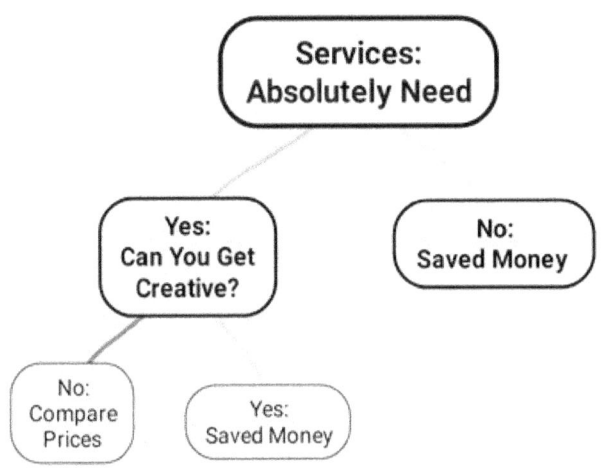

Second Commandment:
Purchase Wholesale

The next expense in your *Wealthy Palm Tree* is the *Wholesale bubble*. If you want to reduce your expenses, then buying products at wholesale prices is critical.

This refers to any <u>physical product that you buy more than once a year,</u> it covers all your basic consumables: laundry detergent, toothpaste, pet food, diapers, lotion, peanut butter, gum, light bulbs, and much more.

Most of these expenses are the things you need to survive and they fall into three major groups: food, household products, and personal care products.

The goal is to buy all these items wholesale and in bulk. Start with trying to buy a supply for 3 months and then work your way up to 6 months and ultimately a full year's worth.

Let me point out that you are not changing *how many units* you buy per year, you're just changing the point in time and the price you pay. This is what Mark Cuban calls *"using the transactional value of cash"*.

If you change from sporadic, impulsive purchases to *strategic wholesale purchases*, you can save more than 30% on your consumables every year. There are very few investments out there with such a guaranteed high return on investment for your dollar.

If you are not yet convinced that buying a year's worth of batteries at wholesale prices is the way to go, then consider these *four benefits*:

1: Places such as Target or Walgreens charge a premium retail price for everything they sell whereas Costco (because of the larger quantities per item) can offer the same items at cheaper wholesale prices. Prices can even decline further if you are able to source online directly from the manufacturer.

Why would you spend unnecessary amounts at Target when you could work toward long-term financial wealth? The key word here is long-term: A onetime purchase at a slightly higher price might not seem that big of a deal. But if you add up all those expenses over the course of a year and then a lifetime, those "onetime purchases" can determine whether you are able to retire a couple years earlier or not.

2: The second benefit of wholesale is that you save on gas and time. When you buy your consumables in bulk and in advance, you have fewer trips to make to the store. The icing on the cake: No more frustration when you run out of deodorant or shaving cream!

3: Fewer trips to the store also eliminates the temptation to buy on impulse for those items you don't need. When you are not at the store, you cannot give in to those alluring offers and amazing deals that scream at you in bright colors.

With fewer "trips and clicks" you are much less likely to fall victim to up-selling strategies that stores (retail and online) strategically put in front of your eyes, or Amazon algorithmically places over your mouse.

4: Last, think of inflation. Product price inflation is more than just the inflation of the dollar. The price inflation principle says that the price of a product either gradually increases over time, or that (should the price stay the same) the amount you receive for that price will be lower. In other words, the price you pay today if you buy something in bulk is the lowest price you will ever pay.

When it comes to buying wholesale, it's all about where you go locally or online. The main locations you will be sourcing your consumables from will be Costco, Sam's Club, eBay, and Amazon – for the really creative – local auctions.

If Walmart is all you have available in your area, that's fine, (even though Walmart is not my preferred choice for bulk-buying) but they do offer price matching of their competitors.

If you want to benefit from this wholesale strategy the most, it is important to think about your storing options at home. It's wonderful to save big dollars on items that will last for months, but if your bathroom cabinet doesn't have room for eight shampoo bottles, ten toothpastes, five laundry detergents, and twenty-two cleaning products, you will get stressed out (naturally).

This is where investing in a shelving unit is crucial: Cleaning products on one shelf, bathroom supplies on the next, and any storable overstock food on another.

Don't forget to be extra careful when buying wholesale. <u>Double-check all products for damage and expiration dates before you buy them.</u> Otherwise, your money saving mission turns into another unnecessary expense, doing nothing for your long-term wealth.

For now, however, it's time to buckle up and get ready for some math, I will keep it as simple as possible so that you don't zone out.

Companies love to trick us with the pricing and sizing of their packaging. Sometimes, without realizing, we choose the more expensive option when comparing different offers. Take a moment and do the math to find out which offer on the same product will save you the most.

In person, it is easier to determine which offer is better because we *see* if we are getting more of a product by buying two 32-ounce bottles for $9 each or one big 75-ounce bottle for $20. But even here we need to cover some basic math.

To calculate if you're making the right choice, take the unit of measurement (this can be ounces, liters, or square feet for products like wrapping paper) and divide it by the cost of each of the two items.

When it comes to online shopping, be extra careful before you click the "Buy Now" button. I'm sure you know this feeling: You order an item online, relying solely on the marketing of the picture, and are highly disappointed when you open the package at home. The item is so different from the pictures online!

To avoid nasty surprises, take the time to read the seller's description, especially on eBay. If you don't, chances are high that you may waste your money unnecessarily.

Looking at the Wealthy Palm Tree, *Wholesale* products are your second-largest expense. When you add them to your *Automated* services, combined they make up close to 80% of your expenses. Hopefully that number makes clear how important it is for you to be conscious of how you are spending your money.

Third Commandment:
Source Below Market Value

This section is focused on the final bubble under the *expenses section*: *Products*. This refers to items you keep for a long period of time, e.g. electronics, baby toys, big boy toys, jewelry, clothes.

These purchases count towards our overall satisfaction and we shouldn't entirely go without them. But if we (keyword: occasionally) indulge ourselves, why not do it the smart way? This section of our expenses is where we have the opportunity to stop being a consumer and start becoming an investor.

When it comes to *Automated, Services, and Wholesale* expenses, we have no choice but to be a consumer and hand our money over to companies, the government (taxes), and banks.

But with items from the *Product* bubble, we do have the opportunity to keep our money and even profit occasionally from our purchases.

For most of these products, there will come a day when you don't need or want them anymore. The electronics become out dated, your taste in jewelry changes, the baby toys are no longer needed.

This is your opportunity to resell these items, striving for $1 = $1 return on your investment so your net worth can stay the same. Only if you're willing to learn how to purchase physical products as an investor.

Even though this seems like a big win, it's not the time for celebration yet. Because the average consumer chooses to buy everything brand new, he or she still loses (or wastes) money no matter how good the deal. After the buyer opens the new box, very rarely will they be able to recoup the full $1. In most cases, the value is slashed in half.

You probably heard the saying "the house always wins". It usually refers to casinos and is based on statistics. However, you can easily apply this saying to the way you are spending your money. See the retail stores, restaurants, and brands are the "house". They always are making money off of you, no matter how much of a "great deal" you think you are getting.

That is the nature of buying second-hand items: People are less willing to pay the full price for a used item, even though it might still be in perfect working condition.

As much as this is a financial problem when you try to resell your own *products*, this is also a blessing when you are on the other end of the trade!

Advertising and marketing have wired our brains and desires to the point that we want to have our items now, brand new, and ideally made by a well-known brand.

These are all reasons why we are happy to pay more money when in actual fact we don't have to. If you are willing to buy it second-hand and prepared to wait for when the price of your desired item is right, saving money is guaranteed!

Learning the ropes of buying (and selling) on Amazon, eBay, Craigslist, or treasure-hunting at thrift stores and garage sales pays off instantly. The main reason why many people are uncomfortable with the idea of hand-me-downs is their ego. If you believe that you or your family are too precious for (oftentimes only slightly) used items, then getting a handle on your financial situation will become impossible.

With today's technology, there is hardly any excuse not to resell your unused or unwanted items online. With a little practice, it can take you less than five minutes to list, sell, and package an item.

Now, personally I take the reselling idea one step further: When I walk into a thrift store I not only purchase an item that I need, but also try to source one or two items that I can flip for a profit online.

This way I use the initial investment to generate more money. I get a great return on both, my money and my time. We will cover this exact strategy shortly in the *Flipping Your Way to Wealth* section.

Another story is holidays and birthdays because you will not be keeping these products. In this case, your strategy is to source the gifts as low-priced as you possibly can.

Get creative, but most importantly: Start early and don't leave the Christmas presents to the last minute. Remember your shelving unit is also a great place to store future gifts when you come across a treasure in mid-September.

Let's clarify this last commandment. <u>Stop buying new from retail stores, period.</u> The house always wins. You don't stand a chance. When you do this, you are letting their business profit off of your warehouse.

Valuing Your Health

When we take a close look at our expenses, we can't ignore those related to our health. Medical bills wipe out financial cushions in the blink of an eye and thus impact our short- and long-term financial situation immensely.

Therefore, part of creating wealth for you and your family entails applying the *Three Spending Commandments* in the best interest of your health. There is no use in short-term savings, for example, on poor-quality food if it means that in the long run you are depleted of nutrients and suffer physically. Be smart and invest in both, your brain and your body.

Condition	Monthly Healthcare Expense Range	Annual Out-of-Pocket Expense
Good Health	$635	$7620
Diabetes	$801-$850	$9612-$10200
Congestive Heart Failure	$901-$950	$10812-$11400
Had a Heart Attack	$1001	$12012

(Source www.medicare.gov)

Flipping

Your

Way to Wealth

The Art of Flipping

I believe that there is one fundamental skill that is required if you want to speed up paying off your debt, and that is learning *The Art of Flipping*.

Flipping is simple, you can virtually flip anything and it doesn't take long to perfect. It's the classic example of investing 101, buying low and selling high. The good news is that technology makes it easy and accessible to everyone.

When dial-up internet was being used, flipping was a lot more complicated. You still were able to sell items on eBay but you had to be very knowledgeable on the value of the vintage piece of jewelry or power tool you found at the garage sale.

Only after you purchased the item, could you go home, boot up the computer, and begin looking at previously sold items. With this method there was always a higher risk of making a mistake and losing money.

Today, with the computer already in your hand, the only thing you need to know is how to correctly research an item and its current reselling value. <u>The risk of any profit loss is lower than ever before, and the speed in which you can turn a quick buck has never been faster.</u>

On the following pages, I will teach you how easy it is to calculate how much "meat is left on the bones" for any item and list it in a manner of minutes.

What if I told you it is even possible to list an item on your phone while in the thrift store, and by the time you get home, have it already sold. This is one of my real-life examples: I have taken a TI-84 calculator I found at Goodwill for $5.99 while searching for a needed blender. I listed the calculator for $62.99 on Amazon from my phone while still in the store. By the time I got home, it had already sold.

I threw some bubble wrap around it, placed it in a packaging sleeve, printed the shipping label, and dropped it off at the post office on my way to work the next morning.

If you have objections to the post office bit of the story, remember that today even standing in line is a thing of the past. With a prepaid shipping label, you just have to drop it off in one of their located bins. It doesn't get any simpler than that.

The reason I'm educating you about *The Art of Flipping* is that it's an additional source of income that requires very little capital and time. Most importantly it integrates perfectly into your new shopping habits that we discussed, in the *Third Spending Commandment,* on sourcing physical products below market value.

While you are out thrift-shopping, scoping out garage sales, or scouring eBay, you have the opportunity to not only find great deals for yourself and your personal warehouse but also the possibility to turn a quick profit.

All this will result in a timely, handsome ROI (Return On Investment) beyond the boring 8% return the stock market gives you on average over the course of a year. No matter how much you invest, the returns can be amazing. On the calculator mentioned above, I made a staggering 786% ROI on my $5.99 initial investment in just one day.

Sold Price	+$62.99
Purchase Price	-$5.99
Shipping Cost	-$4.85
Amazon Fees	-$5.04
Profit	**+$47.11**

I suggest starting small with a couple of dollars, take the profits and keep turning them over. You can then move to bigger and more expensive items as your experience and capital grow (e.g. cars, campers, motorcycles, and trailers). The more you get the hang of flipping products online, the larger your profits will become.

My top flip to date was on a Dollar Tag Day at Goodwill, where items with a certain color tags on Thursdays are just a dollar. I found a Krups Beertender Heineken keg dispenser on a lower shelf, tucked away in the back. It just happened to have a blue color tag, the color of the day. <u>From the initial $1 investment I ended up selling it on Amazon three weeks later for a whopping $274.95! After fees, I profited $202.06 giving me an insane ROI of 20,206%.</u> Of course, this was a unicorn find, and is not typical, but deals like this are certainly out there.

Three Types of Flips

There are three ways you can flip items to increase your revenue.

1: Flip items that are just lying around your house. Most of us have plenty of these in all corners of our house and garage. They are stranded inventory that have been sitting around for years, decreasing in value and not adding to our wealth. Your own items are the easiest to begin flipping.

2: Flip items you are replacing or that have broken. If you're not already doing this start now, as these items can easily account for an extra thousand dollars a year. Don't just throw items out. Just because something is broken doesn't mean it is worthless. Even broken items can be stripped for parts which you can resell. In some cases, you may even get more for the parts than for the item as a whole.

3: Flip items for profit. When you've learned to do this, you can create a solid side income. When I moved to Phoenix, AZ, the market and timing in my life allowed me to flip full-time. This book isn't necessarily telling you to do that, nor do I want you to, because flipping isn't something that's completely scalable. But when it comes to understanding best use of capital and getting the highest ROI, it is by far one of the best forms of investing.

<u>Remember nearly anything and everything can be flipped for a profit.</u> Use any chance you have to go out and look for items to resell. For example, you can go on a hunt when your kids are at soccer practice. Even if you don't find anything, you are likely to learn what to look for with every trip.

When it comes to setting up a sellers account and fine-tuning the details, it's a lot easier to visually show you the ropes within the available online course at KISSFinicials.com. I include a download of my top most profitable products that I have flipped over the years. The monetary value of this .pdf alone is worth a lot, but as a beginner its greatest value comes from how quickly it shortens your learning curve on finding your first profitable items.

The main platforms for flipping are Amazon and eBay, with a little bit of Craigslist for any of your bigger items (e.g. furniture) that you are unable to ship. Amazon sales are straight up staggering and keep growing at enormous rates. They have made listing and selling items very easy. EBay is also improving and is still acquiring a growing number of customers every day. With both platforms' growth, your chances of selling products successfully grow as well.

We have already talked about the importance of knowing the profitable resell value of your product. Amazon and eBay make the price research a lot easier. On eBay, you can go to *sold listings* to even check the last date when and for how much your product was last sold.

Amazon provides an *Amazon Sellers Ranking* chart which allows you to see what top percentage your product falls under within a certain category. They also include a calculator to make estimating your potential profit a breeze.

Amazon.com
Sales Rank %
Chart

As of 04/01/17
Courtesy of Full-Time FBA

Full-Time
FBA

turn part-time hours into a full-time
income via Amazon FBA

Category	Total Items	Top 1%	Top 3%	Top 5%	Top 10%
APPLIANCES	1,398,938	13,989	41,968	69,947	139,894
ARTS & CRAFTS & SEWING	2,878,899	28,769	86,367	143,945	287,890
AUTOMOTIVE	17,302,066	173,021	519,062	866,103	1,730,206
BABY	1,742,048	17,420	52,261	87,102	174,205
BEAUTY	1,910,636	19,106	67,316	95,627	191,064
BOOKS	62,946,070	629,461	1,888,382	3,147,304	6,294,607
CAMARA & PHOTO	2,012,431	20,124	60,373	100,622	201,243
CDS & VINYL	7,846,947	78,469	236,408	392,347	784,695
CELL PHONE & ACCESS	25,627,917	256,279	766,829	1,276,376	2,562,791
CLOTHING, SHOES, & JEWELRY	39,676,978	396,760	1,182,279	1,978,799	3,967,698
COLLECTIBLES & FINE ART	13,269,162	132,692	398,076	663,468	1,326,916
COMPUTERS & ACESS	9,926,778	99,268	297,773	496,289	992,678
ELECTRONICS	38,999,338	393,993	1,180,980	1,967,967	3,934,934
GROCERY & GOURMET FOOD	1,010,998	10,110	30,330	50,550	101,100
HANDMADE	730,127	7301	21,904	36,606	73,013
HEALTH & PERSONAL CARE	4,961,651	49,617	148,850	248,083	496,165
HOME & KITCHEN	61,526,807	615,268	1,545,804	2,576,340	6,152,681
INDUSTRIAL & SCIENTIFIC	19,618,927	196,189	588,568	980,946	1,961,892
LUGGAGE & TRAVEL GEAR	950,681	9,507	28,520	47,634	95,068
LUXURY BEAUTRY	8,767	88	263	438	877
MOVIES & TV	1,698,766	16,988	47,963	79,938	199,877
MUSICAL INSTRUMENTS	689,103	6,891	17,993	29,286	68,910
OFFICE PRODUCTS	6,401,101	64,011	162,033	270,066	640,110
PATIO, LAWN & GARDEN	2,841,972	28,420	86,269	142,099	284,197
PET SUPPLIES	1,049,024	10,490	31,471	52,951	104,902
SOFTWARE	348,383	3,484	10,451	17,419	34,838
SPORTS & OUTDOORS	21,886,577	218,866	666,597	1,094,329	2,188,658
TOOLS & HOME IMPROVEMENT	10,792,416	107,924	323,772	539,621	1,079,242
TOYS & GAMES	4,771,127	47,711	143,134	238,566	477,113
VIDEO GAMES	462,821	4,628	13,885	23,141	46,282
WINE	8,041	80	241	402	804

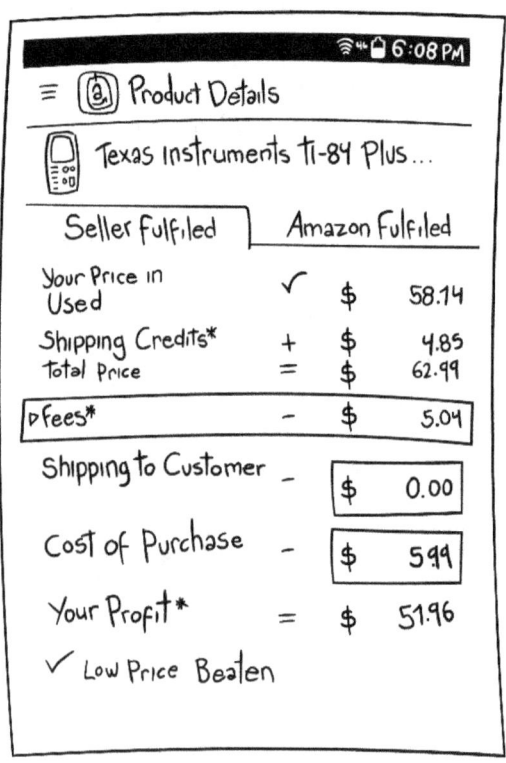

So, make sure to keep your eyes open next time you go shopping, you never know what treasure you will find and flip next.

Your Income Has No Limit

It's our income that has no limit. Yet we don't spend near the same amount of time trying to generate more income. It's easier to 10X our income then it is to 1/10th our expenses. Unless, of course, we are keen on selling our house for one of those tiny homes or trade our car in for an electric moped and live our lives rolling the dice every day without insurance.

Sure, a tiny home sounds exciting for the first couple of months but long-term? As ESPN says it best, "C'MON, MAN." Instead, we remain passive and *hope* for that raise. *Hope* that our investments double. *Hope* to receive a huge inheritance.

Your job is your main stream of income right now. So, you need to pay equal attention to that area of your life, no matter how desperate you are to quit and generate money another way. You need to treat your salary as if it was a stock in the stock market.

Times have changed, and the paper resume can only do so much. A polished online presence is increasingly important. Employers scan through social media and LinkedIn to get a feel for you as a potential employee before they invite you to an interview. That is part of their due diligence.

In order to improve your chances of increasing your salary, you need a strong online presence with a solid network. Start connecting with people on LinkedIn, for example, *before* you search for a new job.

If you decide you would like to stay with your current employer, be clear about the points that impact your success – before you even think of negotiating your salary.

What you can control: your approach, the confidence you have when negotiating, how prepared you are in terms of research you have done, your value to the company, and so on.

Depending on your boss's response and previous raises you have received (or not), strongly consider if the company you are working for right now is a growing company. Be watchful, especially in the years when the market is up.

Look behind the curtain of promising-sounding speeches and newsletters and check if they are compensating the hard-working employees adequately.

It turns out that every action you take towards increasing your income means the world when it comes to paying off your debt. <u>When you "stack" the *Wealthy Palm Tree*, the *Art of Flipping,* and an increase in your salary, for example, the results you can see in a short amount of time can be astonishing.</u>

Problems to Profits

Life will undoubtedly keep throwing curveballs your way, challenges that only seem to accumulate when you already are in a difficult financial situation. We all go through them, you are never alone.

The bigger the problem, the greater the chance one can't find the solution on their own. Everyone will get to a point where they need someone to help them over an obstacle. Why not try to be that someone that holds the solution?

<u>With so many people wrestling with the same problems as you, know there is always someone willing to pay for a solution.</u> All you have to do is be proactive, and bring that solution to them. With the power of the internet and the increasing number of users, this opportunity has never been easier to achieve.

These aren't just empty words to motivate you to focus on your problem-solving abilities; this is something that has happened many times before. Take a look at the world around you <u>– all great things you see were created to help people overcome one obstacle or another.</u> This is why today, we the modern human, have so many products that we use on a daily basis.

In order to go from being in debt to reaching financial stability, you're going to have to change the way you approach your problems in life. When you start changing the way you think, you will start changing the way you live.

"Money is nothing more than a reflection of your creativity, your capacity to focus, and your ability to add value and receive back. If you can find a way to create value – that is, add value for a massive number of people – you will have an opportunity to have a massive amount of economic abundance in your life."

– Robbins, Tony. Money:
Master the Game, 2014, p. 193

History Never

Repeats Itself,

Man Does

Herd Mentality

We are all part of one giant herd, mankind, and our minds are programmed to put the wellbeing of the herd above our own. Evolutionarily speaking, it makes sense because this used to be the only way we were able to survive.

Even today, to a lesser degree, of course, <u>we rely on the behavioral patterns of others to decide when to run, fight, keep quiet, or when to rebel.</u> That is why we only tend to take action when we are certain that others will follow and support us.

We are quick to adapt to this behavior of the herd, and what the majority of the herd does become, over time, part of our everyday lives. For better or worse, and hardly ever questioned by anyone.

You only have to look at our current economic situation – the majority of people spend a great portion of life battling debt. <u>Considering the time and effort we put into "making" money, we get surprisingly little in return.</u>

"Over the course of our lives, the average American pays more than half of his or her income to an assortment of taxes: income tax, property tax, sales tax, tax at the pump and so on. (According to what many experts estimate, currently, that's 54.25 cents per dollar.)

The fact is, on average, approximately one-third of the income you have left after taxes will be spent on paying down interest! That leaves you with (drum roll, please) whopping 28.5% of your hard-earned income left over to pay for everything else in life."
– Robbins, Tony. Money: Master the Game, 2014, p. 275

"1. You work for someone else. Most people, working for a paycheck, are making the owner, or the shareholders richer. Your efforts and success will help provide for the owner's success and retirement.

2. You work for the government. The government takes its share from your paycheck before you even see it. By working harder, you simply increase the amount of taxes taken by the government – most people work from January to May just for the government.

3. You work for the bank. After taxes, your next largest expense is usually your mortgage and credit card debt."

*- Kiyosaki, Robert T. Rich Dad,
Poor Dad, 2004, p. 72.*

These statements can easily be applied to the life of any herd, including ours. But why do we still calmly continue to work for someone else? What happens when the herd wakes up?

Big League Chew

As some major historical events show, the herd often lacks common sense, <u>and most individuals of the herd put little thought into their actions as long as they correspond with the actions of the rest of the herd.</u>

This is the reason why we are prone to make terrible financial decisions, and why it is so important to educate ourselves. If we don't, the consequences can be devastating, dangerous even. At times, our society might be slow to react, but when people see the value in something it is only a matter of time before the herd starts to invest. Why? Because <u>they all want their piece of the proverbial pie.</u>

However, they often realize too late that the pie is only not big enough for everyone but that, sometimes, it is not even there to begin with.

An excellent example of this herd mentality is the creation of bubbles and the subsequent market crashes. Before we move on to some more recent examples, let me first explain what these two things are.

<u>Economic or asset bubbles are characterized by rapid and high increases in the price of an asset far beyond its actual value.</u> Bubbles are created by investors who put a lot of money into an asset to the point that they not only increase the demand but also the price. This then makes the asset seem much more valuable than it really is.

The herd mentality comes into play when more and more investors start doing the same. Very soon, countless people who think they are using a golden opportunity to make a profit in actual fact put money into something that has little to no chance of generating a return.

As is the case with any bubble, they keep expanding until there is no other alternative but to burst. When that happens and the bubble in question is big enough, the consequences oftentimes are disastrous.

The market crashes and the previously overinflated value of the asset drops at lightning speed. When investors realize that they can't expect any more returns on their investment, they start to massively sell their stocks in an attempt to minimize losses.

The two most recent bubbles are the dotcom and the housing bubble. Following the rise of the commercial use of the Internet, i.e. the appearance of the "dotcoms" or commercial websites, investors rushed to participate in the mania with unrealistic expectations and without proper analysis of the situation.

However, the majority of dotcoms failed to reach the expected value. The dotcom bubble burst and made way for a new recession.

The financial crisis of 2008 created the biggest disruption to the U.S. housing market since the Great Depression. This severely affected almost every household. Not only did home prices drop nearly thirty percent but the stock market took a fifty percent tumble from its highs.

"What's the simple and core investment lesson here? What goes up will come down! Ray Dalio told me point-blank that in your lifetime 'it's almost certain that whatever you're going to put your money in, there will come a day when you will lose fifty percent to seventy percent.' Yikes!"

– Robbins, Tony. Money: Master the Game, 2014, p. 299

Bubbles and the subsequent crashes can lead to a depression that takes an economy years, if not decades, to fully recover. <u>Just remember: Because the herd is running towards a cliff, burning their money, doesn't mean you have to follow.</u>

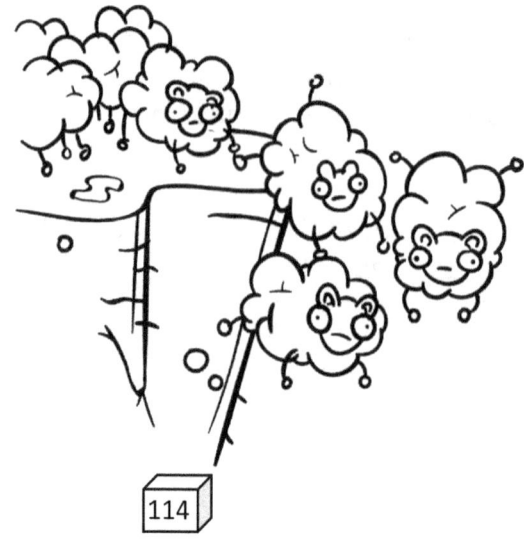

Stock Pickers
and
Wine Tasters

What do stock pickers and wine tasters have in common? They both give expert advice on things the general public knows very little about: stocks and quality wines. But how accurate is their advice, and is it even necessary?

A study led by a researcher at the University of Bordeaux asked 57 experts to try and describe two wines, one white and one red. The experts tasted the wines and all came to similar conclusions – the red wine was "intense, deep, and spicy" and the white wine "lively, fresh, and floral." These are the most common descriptions used by wine tasters when it comes to red and white wine.

Now, that wouldn't be so unusual if the wines they tasted hadn't both been the same white wine. The "red wine" had been colored with red food coloring. None of the expert wine tasters tasted the difference (or lack thereof) and they all gave their expert opinion which turned out to be generic descriptions usually associated with red or white wines.

Expert stock pickers aren't all that different when it comes to selecting stocks that would make a good investment. Why? Because the majority of experts, just as any layman, can't pick stocks that beat the market average. Nearly 96% of actively managed mutual funds fail to beat the market over any sustained period of time.

"The goal of the nonprofessional should not be to pick winners – neither he nor his "helpers" can do that - but should rather be to own a cross-section of businesses that aggregate and are bound to do well. A low-cost S&P 500 index fund will achieve this goal."
– Warren Buffet

"When you look at the results on an after-fee, after-tax basis, over reasonably long periods of time, there's almost no chance that you end up beating the index fund." – David Swensen

— IMPACT OF FEES —

$1 Million Invested
8% assumed annualized return over 30 years

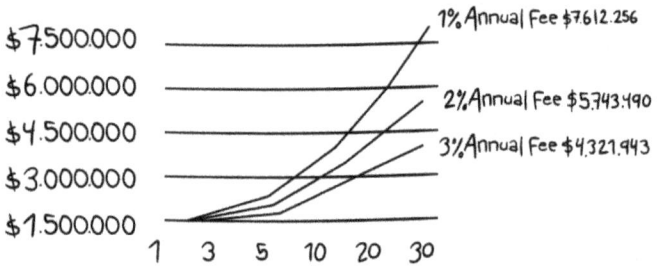

$7.500.000	1% Annual Fee $7,612.256
$6.000.000	2% Annual Fee $5,743,490
$4.500.000	3% Annual Fee $4,321,943
$3.000.000	
$1.500.000	

1   3   5   10   20   30

Time in Years

We think that anyone with the word "expert" next to their job description is the ultimate authority on the subject. Even though most of them are, your life decisions should not solely depend on them. Through education, persistence, and consistency, you can be your own financial expert.

It is your money, after all. If you can earn it, you can just as easily control it. A great source for learning about the stock market and investing principle is what I consider the financial bible, "Money: Master the Game!" by Tony Robbins.

Mindset,

Knowledge,

Action

Mindset

Achieving your goals is based on three key elements: <u>Mindset, Knowledge, and Action</u>. If you understand and apply these elements, in this order, you will be able to visualize your objectives and goals in life.

The significance of a positive mindset has already been explained. It takes small steps on the long journey towards your goal, that change is fundamental. A different attitude toward your situation will help you let go of the negativity that is holding you back and instead will open your mind to more drive and determination.

But where do you find the strength to change your mindset when it's lacking motivation? For one, there are countless inspirational and motivational speeches available online. Browse Youtube and create your own personal "motivation playlist".

Any time you don't feel like getting up, going to work, exercising, or working on yourself, play the videos from your list. It is hard to hit the snooze button when the people on the screen are full of energy and practically scream at you to get moving.

While those videos are great to pick you up when motivation is low, they won't do the trick in the long run. External drivers never do. Your drive to turn your financial situation around has to come from within if it's to be successful.

This is why continual self-education is important. It equips you with the tools you need to succeed. Remember: Knowledge is king.

"As a child, my dad often told us that the Japanese were aware of three powers: "The power of the sword, the jewel, and the mirror.
The sword symbolizes the power of weapons. America has spent trillions of dollars on weapons and, because of this, is the supreme military presence in the world.
The jewel symbolizes the power of money. There is some degree of truth to the saying, "Remember the golden rule. He who has the gold makes the rules."
The mirror symbolizes the power of self-knowledge. This self-knowledge, according to Japanese legend, was the most treasured of the three."
- Kiyosaki, Robert T.
Rich Dad, Poor Dad, 2004, p. 35.

Knowledge

> "The best investment you can make is an investment in yourself... The more you learn, the more you'll earn." Warren Buffett

The way we approach a new board game is very similar to the average individual beginning to invest his or her money. The "experienced" parents or friends lay out their versions of how the financial game is played. They explain the rules and throw in their own experiences, mistakes they have made, and maybe even some tricks that you the new investor needs to be aware of.

In the end, however, all that a new player gets from such a vast amount of information is confusion. Of course, knowing the rules of investing is important but it is the knowledge and experience you gather yourself that counts the most.

Only when a beginner sees experienced investors at work can he or she truly understand how the game is played. And it is only when they try their hand at the financial game themselves that they acquire valuable experience.

One of the most recognized resources successful investors mention over and over are their mentors. This is true for almost anyone who is considered successful in his field, and the value of mentorship goes beyond the pure dedication of time.

A mentor gives direction, practical advice, and sometimes even access to his or her network. If you have a potential mentor in mind, be very deliberate about your approach and outline what you can offer in return to make it a mutually beneficial interaction.

On top of the personal mentor-mentee-relationship, technology gives you access to a variety of successful entrepreneurs, speakers, coaches, and established entrepreneurs you can learn from, day and night. Again, I highly recommend Youtube as your source of choice. Listen and absorb the free content that those people upload; <u>80% of what you do comes down to learning the fundamentals.</u>

As you listen to multiple people, you will notice "patterns" or "stories" that every one of them repeats. That's what you are looking for. They are your golden nuggets of fundamentals you want to follow. So make it a habit to watch and learn the principles of success from the best.

If you are interested in a particular industry or line of products, find out who is successfully doing today what you want to do tomorrow. Read their biographies or blogs, watch their talks and interviews. In short: Follow their path and copy the process/mindset which is working for them. This is your fastest way to get from Point A to Point B.

Sometimes, "buying your way in" is a lot easier than "brown-nosing your way in". Think of the types of courses most of us have taken: college, eLearning online, weekend seminars, etc. Most successful people and teachers have created courses based on their experiences and personal "golden nuggets".

Buying a course saves you a lot of time because information is readily available and laid out in order. No need to scavenger-hunt the web. You will get the most benefit from courses which actively engage you in the learning process, and do so step-by-step.

Just as with information overload from online sources alone, you can get lost in a course that is purely knowledge-based but doesn't equip you with the tools you can apply to your *specific* situation.

"Master a formula and then learn a new one: The power of learning quickly. In order to make bread, every baker follows a recipe, even if it's only held in their head. The same is true for making money. That's why money is often called "dough".

- Kiyosaki, Robert T. *Rich Dad, Poor Dad*, 2004, p. 154

Action

"When someone has the right strategy in front of him, and he still doesn't succeed, it's because he's missing the second key to breakthrough: the power of story.

If you're not taking action and the answer is sitting there in front of you, there's only one reason: you've created a set of beliefs that you've tied into a story- a story about why it won't work, why it can't work why it only works for other people. It's only for the rich, the thin, the lucky, the happy in relationships. It's easy to come up with a limiting story.

But the people who make change happen, who get stuff done, who accomplish, who shift, who grow, who learn, they take their strategy and attach a new story to it: a story of empowerment, a story of "I can and I will" instead of "I can't and I won't" It goes from being a story of limitations to a story of empowerment:

"I will not be one of the many who can't, I will be one of the few who do."

– Robbins, Tony. Money:
Master the Game, 2014, p. 189

Mindset and knowledge can prepare you for what is coming, they can give you vision. But it's only when you take action can you turn your dreams into reality.

"Vision without action is merely a dream.
Action without vision just passes the time.
Vision with action can change the world."
- *Joel Barker*

You now know that changing "how" you spend your money, and not necessarily "how much", is imperative to your long-term success. Just as it is to invest in your education and your health.

I hope that comparing your busy life with the business of running a warehouse under firm management will stick with you. It is absolutely important to learn how to sort out your life first before making further investments or starting a second business.

My main objective was to change your mindset and show you how you can stay organized, spend less and save more without boring spreadsheets and complicated calculations. Every household budget can be replaced by your own *Wealthy Palm Tree*. It is easy to follow as it shows the logic that connects all of your income, assets, and expenses.

Let's be clear about one thing: All the knowledge and lessons of this book won't mean anything if you don't put them into practice. The sooner you apply the *Three Spending Commandments* with the *Art of Flipping*, the quicker you will pay off your debt, and retire early under your own fully shaded *Wealthy Palm Tree*.

Take action today on something that will benefit you far into your future. No more excuses and no more hesitation, for your goals don't know what day it is.

"Less expenses, less work, less stuff, equals more money, more time, more joy."

KISSFinancials.com

Casey Ommen

Bonus Quotes

As a bonus to speed up your learning even further and get your mind thinking as an investor, I have included many quotes that I extracted from each of the four books mentioned below. These are the very golden nuggets that helped me write this book, so I hope you find them just as valuable as I have.

* "Money Mastery" by Tony Robbins
* "Rich Dad, Poor Dad" by Robert Kiyosaki
* "The Total Money Makeover" by Dave Ramsey
* "Why We Want You To Be Rich" by Donald Trump and Robert Kiyosaki

"The human mind is an amazing thing. It's a survival mechanism, so it tends to look for what's wrong, what to avoid, what to look out for. You may have evolved but your brain is still a 2-million-year-old structure, and if you want to be fulfilled and happy, that's not its first priority. You have to take control of it." – Robbins, Tony. *Money: Master the Game, 2014, p. 585*

"Learning that by changing your body first, you can change your mind. I teach many ways to create immediate change in your state, one of the simplest ways is to change what I call your physiology. You can change the way you think by changing the way you move and breathe. Emotion is created by motion. Massive action is the cure to all fear. Think about it, fear is physical. You feel it in your mouth, in your body, in your stomach.

So is courage, and you can move from one to another in a matter of milliseconds if you learn to make radical shifts in the way you move, breathe, speak, and use your physical body. I've used these insights for almost four decades to turn around some of the world's greatest peak-performance athletes, financial traders and business and political leaders... Our bodies are able to change our minds!" – Robbins, Tony. *Money: Master the Game, 2014, p. 197*

"Through education, you gain vision. Through vision, you gain the ability to spot economic problems and turn them into economic opportunities. However, you must be careful about what kind of education you receive." - Trump, Donald, and Robert T Kiyosaki. *Why We Want You To Be Rich*, 2006, p. 81

"Since your mind is your most valuable asset and your most valuable lever, you need to be careful about what you put in it. Sometimes it is even more difficult to get rid of thoughts and ideas that are already in your mind than it is to learn something new." - Trump, Donald, and Robert T Kiyosaki. *Why We Want You To Be Rich*, 2006, p. 119

"So our message to you is the same message we received from our rich dad: "We are all born rich. We all have been given the most powerful lever on earth, our minds... so use your mind for leverage to make you rich rather than to make excuses." - Trump, Donald, and Robert T Kiyosaki. *Why We Want You To Be Rich*, 2006, p. 113

"I guess we all probably heard the term "groupthink" by now. It's that old herd mentality that seems to bring out the best and the worst in people. By the best, I mean that sometimes a shepherd will surface. But that's an unlikely scenario. It's usually the wolves that will surface first, and the herd will be primed and ready to follow. What we're trying to do here is break up the herd before we are incapable of seeing, hearing, thinking and doing for ourselves. People who are capable of thinking for themselves will rarely be part of any herd." - Trump, Donald, and Robert T Kiyosaki. *Why We Want You To Be Rich*, 2006, p. 43

"John Maxwell tells of a study done on monkeys. A group of monkeys was locked in a room with a pole at the center. Some luscious, ripe bananas were placed on top of the pole. When a monkey would begin to climb the pole, the experimenters would knock him off with a blast of water from a fire hose. Each time a monkey would climb, off he would go, until all the monkeys had been knocked off repeatedly, thus learning that the climb was hopeless. The experimenters then observed that the other primates would pull down any monkey trying to climb. They replaced a single monkey with one who didn't know the system. As soon as the new guy tried to climb, the others would pull him down and punish him for trying. One by one, each left in the room that had experienced the fire hose. Still, none of the new guys were allowed to climb. the other monkeys pulled them down. Not one monkey in the room knew why, but none were allowed to get the bananas.

We aren't monkeys, but sometimes we exhibit behavior that seems rather chimplike. We don't even remember why; we just know that debt is needed to win. We are like the last set of monkeys. With rolled eyes, we spout the pat lines associated with the myth as if anyone not wanting to have debt is unintelligent." – Ramsey, Dave. *The Total Money Makeover*, 2007, pp. 19-20

"Albert Einstein defined insanity as "doing the same thing over and over again and expecting different results." In this case, it is my opinion that it is insanity to keep sending kids to school and not teaching them about money." - Trump, Donald, and Robert T Kiyosaki. *Why We Want You To Be Rich*, 2006, pp. 40-41

"Wall Street is the only place that people ride in a Rolls Royce to get advice from those who take the subway." - Trump, Donald, and Robert T Kiyosaki. *Why We Want You To Be Rich*, 2006, p. 73

"One of the riskiest things a person can do is say, "I have $10,000. What should I do with it?" The problem with announcing that you do not know what to do with your money is that it attracts millions of people who do know what to do with your money – take it." - Trump, Donald, and Robert T Kiyosaki. *Why We Want You To Be Rich*, 2006, p. 227

"I talk about how some people do not want to give people fish or teach others to fish... instead, they sell people fish. Many of these people are stockbrokers, real estate brokers, financial planners, bankers and insurance agents.

They are in the business of selling... not necessarily teaching or giving. When you put the two words, sell and fish, together, you get the word selfish. And even though most people in the business may not be selfish, enough are to make the word ring true. I use it here to emphasize the importance of staying on your guard to be aware of the difference between those who give – the teachers – and those who sell.

We are concerned that most people do not choose to learn to manage their own money or learn to invest their own money. Instead of *learning*, they simply *turn* their money over to experts and then hope and pray their experts are truly experts." - Trump, Donald, and Robert T Kiyosaki. *Why We Want You To Be Rich*, 2006, p. 49

"Every day is filled with defining moments. From the moment we wake up, we define ourselves when we decide to get up and exercise or sleep an extra half hour we define ourselves when we call in sick even though we could go to work. We define ourselves when we watch television instead of reading a book on business or investing. And we define ourselves when we turn our money over to a salesperson to invest for us instead of learning to invest for ourselves." - Trump, Donald, and Robert T Kiyosaki. *Why We Want You To Be Rich*, 2006, p. 28

"I'd like to emphasize the importance of studying history. Knowledge is power. We can learn from history, from the civilizations and empires that have made up the history of the world thus far." - Trump, Donald, and Robert T Kiyosaki. *Why We Want You To Be Rich*, 2006, p. 83

"Everything that happens once can never happen again. But everything that happens twice will surely happen a third time." - Coelho, Paulo. *The Alchemist*, 2014, p. 161

"It's better to learn from history than to repeat the same blunders. As the old saying goes, "Those who haven't learned from history are destined to repeat it." - Trump, Donald, and Robert T Kiyosaki. *Why We Want You To Be Rich*, 2006, p. 83

"The worst thing is to learn hard lessons by doing before learning. Learning in itself is an investment. Robert and I are trying to bring that home to you in an accessible way.
Rules aren't always pleasant, but unless you're in a position to change the rules, laws, and constraints, it's a good idea to know about them." - Trump, Donald, and Robert T Kiyosaki. *Why We Want You To Be Rich*, 2006, p. 79

"History also teaches us that debt wasn't always a way of life; in fact, three of the biggest lenders today were founded by people who hated debt. Sears now makes more money on credit than on the sale of merchandise. They are not a store; they are a lender with some stuff out front.

However, in 1910 Sears catalog stated, "Buying on Credit Is Folly." J.C. Penney department stores make millions annually on their plastic, but their founder was nicknamed James "Cash" Penny because he detested the use of debt. Henry Ford thought debt was a lazy man's method to purchase items, and his philosophy was so ingrained in Ford Motor Company that Ford didn't offer to finance until ten years after General Motors did. Now, of course, Ford Motor Credit is one of the most profitable of Ford Motor's operations. The old school saw that folly of debt; the new school saw the opportunity to take advantage of the consumer with debt." – Ramsey, Dave. *The Total Money Makeover*, 2007, p. 23

"A few years back, Mattel put out "Cool Shopping Barbie," which was sponsored by MasterCard. Of course, this "cool" babe had her own MasterCard. When she scanned her card, the cash register said, "Credit approved." There was so much consumer backlash that Mattel pulled the product. This year, Barbie came out with the "Barbie Cash Register," and apparently this lady does a lot of shopping. The register comes with its own American Express card. Why are these companies selling to our small children? Kid-branding intends to influence card choices later in life." – Ramsey, Dave. *The Total Money Makeover*, 2007, p. 47

"It's not what you earn that matters, it's what you keep. Our third strategy for speeding things up is to get more money out of your investments by reducing your fees and taxes, and reinvesting the difference." – Robbins, Tony. *Money: Master the Game, 2014, p. 273*

"You must pay taxes. But there's no law that says you gotta leave a tip." – Morgan Stanley advertisement – Robbins, Tony. *Money: Master the Game, 2014, p. 273*

"Compound interest is such a powerful tool that Albert Einstein once called it the most important invention in all of human history." – Robbins, Tony. *Money: Master the Game, 2014, p. 50*

"Like it or not, all of us are in this game of money. Regardless of whether you are rich or poor, living in the United States, Asia, Europe, Africa, South America, Canada or wherever, we are all in this game of money." - Trump, Donald, and Robert T Kiyosaki. *Why We Want You To Be Rich*, 2006, pp. 122

"If something is going to affect your life, it's best to know as much as you can about it." - Trump, Donald, and Robert T Kiyosaki. *Why We Want You To Be Rich*, 2006, p. 127

"To spend your life living in fear, never exploring your dreams, is cruel. To work hard for money, thinking that money will buy you things that will make you happy is also cruel. To wake up in the middle of the night terrified about paying bills is a horrible way to live. To live a life dictated by the size of a paycheck is not really a life. Thinking that a job will make you feel secure is lying to yourself. That's cruel, and that's the trap I want you to avoid, if possible. I've seen how money runs people's lives. Don't let that happen to you. Please don't let money run your life." - Kiyosaki, Robert T. *Rich Dad, Poor Dad*, 2004, p. 41.

"Riskless return and Kyle Bass. "The famed hedge fund guru, with one of the biggest wins of the last century, used his hard-earned money to buy... well, money: $2 million in nickels- enough to fill up a small room. What gives? While a nickel's value fluctuates, at the time of this interview Kyle told me, "Tony, the US nickel is worth about 6.8 cents today in its 'melt value'. That means 5 cents is really worth 6.8 cents [36% more] in its true metal value." – Robbins, Tony. *Money: Master the Game, 2014, p. 174*

"Superficially, I think it looks like entrepreneurs have a high tolerance for risk. But one of the most important phrases in my life is "protect the downside". – Richard Branson"

"I'm not really into etymology, but recently it was discovered that the most used word in the English language is "Time." "Money" may have been in the top 100, but it was nowhere near "Time" in the ratings. Then I remembered how someone once explained life as a credit card that's given to us at birth – minus the expiration date. The time we have on that card becomes the big question, not the money. The properties of time have always been of great interest to physicists and scientists. Time is measured by numbers. Which brings us to math. Which brings us to money. But if you've run out of time - all money in the world won't change that situation." - Trump, Donald, and Robert T Kiyosaki. *Why We Want You To Be Rich*, 2006, p. 127

"How does this apply to investing and finance? Actually, it applies to everything that you do with your time is a very big subject, because lost time can never be recaptured. Very often, lost money can be regained. As Plutarch said, "Time is the wisest of all counselors." In short, be careful of your time and learn to invest it – thoughtfully." - Trump, Donald, and Robert T Kiyosaki. *Why We Want You To Be Rich*, 2006, p. 128

"Getting back to the difference between a saver and an investor, there is one word that separates them, and that word is *leverage*. One definition of leverage is *the ability to do more with less*." - Trump, Donald, and Robert T Kiyosaki. *Why We Want You To Be Rich*, 2006, p. 106

"So if you're wondering why we would take time to talk about the future and technological breakthroughs in a financial book, it's because technology is a hidden asset that every day is compounding its capacity to enrich your life. Also, learning about these trends in technologies can awaken you to some of the greatest investment opportunities of your lifetime." – Robbins, Tony. *Money: Master the Game, 2014, p. 549*

"One of the key secrets if you really want to become wealthy: get in front of a trend." – Robbins, Tony. *Money: Master the Game, 2014, p. 270*

"America as a country and many Americans are in financial trouble because they have not been able to increase the cash flowing into their income column and have lost control over the cash flowing out of their expense column. Also, rather than creating assets, they continually create more liabilities, which accelerates the cash flowing out through the expense column. Someone who has excessive credit card debt takes out a home equity loan to pay off the credit cards, and then goes out and gets into more credit card debt is an example of someone who has lost control." - Trump, Donald, and Robert T Kiyosaki. *Why We Want You To Be Rich, 2006, p. 238*

"The best myth is the "build your credit" myth. Bankers, car dealers, and unknowledgeable mortgage lenders have told America for years to "build your credit." This myth means we have to get debt so we can get more debt because debt is how we get stuff." – Ramsey, Dave. *The Total Money Makeover*, 2007, p. 38

"Some of you are so immature that you are unwilling to delay pleasure for a greater result. I will show you exactly how to get the result you want, so the price you pay will not be in vain. I don't want to walk across hot coals because it is fun, but if I can be shown how a short, painful walk will do away with the lifetime of worry, frustration, stress, and fear that being constantly broke brings me, then bring on the hot coals." – Ramsey, Dave. *The Total Money Makeover*, 2007, p. 6

"As your cash flow grows, you can buy some luxuries. An important distinction is that rich people buy luxuries last, while the poor and middle class tend to buy luxuries first. The poor and the middle class often buy luxury items such as big houses, diamonds, furs, jewelry or boats because they want to look rich. They look rich, but in reality, they just get deeper in debt on credit. The old-money people, the long-term rich, built their asset column first. Then, the income generated from the asset column bought their luxuries. The poor and middle class buy luxuries with their own sweat, blood and children's inheritance. A true luxury is a reward for investing in and developing a real asset." - Kiyosaki, Robert T. *Rich Dad, Poor Dad*, 2004, p. 82.

"An asset is something that puts money into my pocket.
A liability is something that takes money out of my pocket.

This is really all you need to know. If you want to be rich, simply spend your life buying assets. If you want to belong to the poor or middle class, spend your life buying liabilities. It's not knowing the difference that causes most of the financial struggle in the real world." - Kiyosaki, Robert T. *Rich Dad, Poor Dad*, 2004, p. 55.

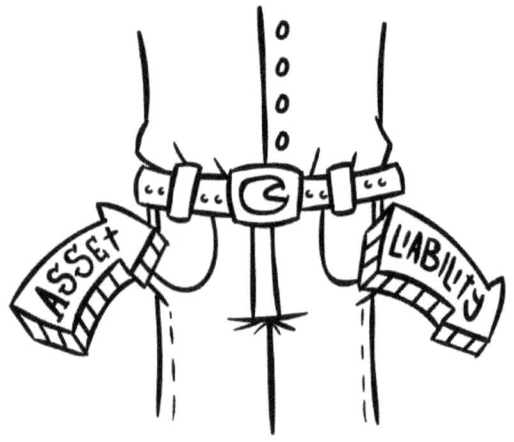

"The Tax Code of the United States also allows other ways to save on taxes. Most of these vehicles are available to anyone, but it is the rich who usually look for them because they are minding their own business. For example, "1031" is jargon for Section 1031 of the Internal Revenue Code, which allows a seller to delay paying taxes on a piece of real estate that is sold for a capital gain through an exchange for a more expensive piece of real estate.

Real estate is one investment vehicle that allows such great tax advantage. As long as you keep trading up in value, you will not be taxed on the gains, until you liquidate. People who do not take advantage of these tax savings offered legally are missing a great opportunity to build their asset column." - Kiyosaki, Robert T. *Rich Dad, Poor Dad*, 2004, p. 91.

Proverbs 22:7: "The rich rules over the poor, and the borrower is servant to the lender." (NKJV). – Ramsey, Dave. *The Total Money Makeover*, 2007, p. 22

"The lesson is that while it is fine to *give* money to friends in need if you have it, loaning them money will mess up relationships." – Ramsey, Dave. *The Total Money Makeover*, 2007, p. 25

"Instead of walking away with a solid financial education, most kids leave school – some already deeply in debt – prepared only to work hard, save money, get out of debt, invest for the long-term and diversify.
Warren Buffett says the following about diversification:
"Diversification is protection against ignorance. It makes very little sense if you know what you are doing." - Trump, Donald, and Robert T Kiyosaki. *Why We Want You To Be Rich*, 2006, p. 41

"Again, there are multiple meaning for the word "diversify." Generally, it means not putting all of your eggs in one basket, which is what Warren Buffett does. To this, I once heard him say, "Keep all your eggs in one basket, but watch the basket closely." Personally, I do not diversify, at least not in the way the financial planners recommend. I do not buy a lot of different assets. I would rather focus. In fact, the way I get ahead is by focusing, not diversifying. One of the better definitions of the word "focus" I have heard is using the word as an acronym:

F = Follow
O = One
C = Course
U = Until
S = Successful" - Trump, Donald, and Robert T Kiyosaki. *Why We Want You To Be Rich*, 2006, p. 110

"The reason I am so passionate about you getting rid of debt is that I have seen how many people make huge strides toward being a millionaire in the short time after they get rid of their payments. If you didn't have a car payment, a student loan, credit cards out your ears, medical debt, or even a mortgage, you could become wealthy very quickly." – Ramsey, Dave. *The Total Money Makeover*, 2007, p. 109

The Secret

"Land was wealth 300 years ago. So the person who owned the land owned the wealth. Then, it was factories and production, and America rose to dominance. The industrialist owned the wealth. Today, it is information and the person who has the most timely information owns the wealth. The problem is, information flies all around the world at the speed of light. The new wealth cannot be contained by boundaries and borders as land and factories were. The changes will be faster and more dramatic. There will be a dramatic increase in the number of new multimillionaires. There also will be those who are left behind."

- Kiyosaki, Robert T. *Rich Dad, Poor Dad*, 2004, p. 101.

Palm Tree

Publishing

151